MW01625118
celebrate
create
joy
welcome
grow
love

WONDERS OF THE *heart*

Gary Hogg

IRIS & EMILY BOOKS

This is a work of nonfiction. Some of the names have been changed for privacy purposes.

This book may be purchased in bulk for educational, business or fund raising use. For information, contact Iris & Emily Books.
(801) 668-5332
irisandemily.com

Book design by Mariah Rupp.
Special thanks to Leslie Stitt, Jeff Good, Shaelee Booth and Sherry Wallwork.

ISBN 978-0-930771-50-8
Printed and bound in the USA.

For Sterling Sky.
My heart grew two sizes the day you were born.

Table of Contents

When you hook your brain to your heart,
you are twice as smart.
— GH

Introduction

Two months into the coronavirus pandemic I was on a hike with my wife, Emily, on North Arm Trail in the mountain valley where we live when I spotted a heart rock. Emily has collected heart rocks for as long as I have known her. This one was pure white and in the perfect shape of a two-inch-tall heart. I picked it up and showed it to her.

"That might be the best one I've ever seen," she commented.

"I know," I replied as I slipped it into my pocket.

A mile further up the trail we spotted a hiker coming toward us. Emily has more friends than anyone I've ever known, and this woman was one of them.

"Hi, Jennifer," Emily called out.

Jennifer was happy to see Emily and they started talking. After catching up about kids and pets, the conversation veered to the pandemic. Jennifer explained that she was struggling. She felt lonely due to the isolation required by social distancing. On top of that, the divisive mood among some in the community left her without a sense of hope.

"You'll think I'm dumb, but today I'm on this trail looking for a heart rock," said Jennifer. "They've always been a sign to me that God is mindful of where I am and what I'm going through. I really need that feeling today."

Without hesitating I reached into my pocket and pulled out the pure white heart rock.

"You can have this one. I found it on the trail this morning," I said.

"We've been carrying it for you," said Emily.

Jennifer began to cry as she took the stone.

"This means more to me than you'll ever know. It's not just a rock. It's a message of hope, hand-delivered by two angels," she said. "You're the reason I am on this trail. I was meant to meet you today."

A simple heart shape found in nature had specific meaning to Jennifer. It eased her mind and strengthened her resolve. It lifted her spirits and restored her hope.

On my subsequent daily hikes I often thought about Jennifer and the heart rock. How did a rock have so much power in her life? Then I realized she wasn't just looking for a heart rock. She was searching for a heart story. She needed a narrative that she could repeat when she felt discouraged.

I believe that Emily and I were meant to be part of that story. I'm sure Jennifer would have found a heart rock that day without our help, but then we wouldn't have had her in our story. And it was our part of the story that led to the creation of this book.

After that day on North Arm Trail, I began looking for heart shapes on my hikes. I found hearts peeking through the clouds, nestled in mountain creeks, frozen in snow and ice, blooming in flowers, and growing in trees. No two of them were the same. Each one was profound in its own way. I photographed them just as I found them. None of the photos were manufactured or contrived. Some were easy to spot while others required a closer look. They were the inspiration for this book.

I found significance in these gifts from Mother Nature. I wondered what I could learn from their stories. What does a heart shaped bubble in a stream tell me about how fragile life is? What is there to learn from a million snowflakes gathering on a branch in the perfect shape of a heart? How can a billowy heart shaped cloud serve as a lesson in finding peace? The skeptic would say it is all random, just as everything in life is. But I'm not a skeptic. These hearts had messages for me. Like a songwriter putting words to someone else's melody, I wrote what each heart conveyed to me. Those verses became the voice of this book.

I couldn't have written these words as a younger man. They are words that were born from experience and life lessons lived and learned. We all have stories that serve as memory markers and make us who we are. These are the personal tales that give our life perspective and meaning. As you read this book, you'll become acquainted with some of the people and events that made me who I am. I have changed some of the names of the participants for privacy reasons. These funny, tender, inspiring stories provide the framework of this book.

This book invites you to find your own path using your heart for a guide. It is a reminder that your existence is part of nature's grand tapestry of life. You are a rare and noted creature in the universe. Your potential to give and accept is as vast as the sky.

Always Best,

Gary

A stick ends up in the shape of a heart. Is it an inspiring miracle of nature or a disappointing piece of unusable wood? Life is full of unexplained moments and surprise endings. One person's disappointment is someone else's opportunity of a lifetime. You get to decide if something is a gift or a gaffe. Always choose to see the miracles.

Living in Color

Each of my children began traveling with me to my speaking engagements at an early age. Those were days of bonding that helped me form valuable relationships with each of my children. Their companionship changed what would be boring road trips into fun adventures.

As they grew into teenagers their eagerness to be my sidekick waned a bit, but they were still willing to travel with me if the speaking engagement was on their list of desired locations.

For my son Jonah, Las Vegas was top of the list. The hotels have nice swimming pools and never-ending buffets. When he was sixteen years old, he agreed to come with me to Las Vegas for a young authors conference. The participants ranged in age from kindergarten to high school and were all blind.

I was asked to kick off the daylong festivities by giving a keynote address and doing some storytelling. Immediately, I knew it was going to be a wonderful day. The students were engaged and loved to laugh. Their enthusiasm was infectious.

After the storytelling session I was invited to spend the rest of the day participating in the scheduled events and making friends with the young authors. By midmorning, Jonah and Seth, a rambunctious third grader, had become fast friends. They joked and laughed as we made our way from each of the scheduled workshops.

Lunch had a beach party theme and was held in the park that connected to the conference venue. Surfer music boomed and pizza was served. Jonah's new friend was in a party mood as he devoured two huge slices of pepperoni pizza.

To make the beach party complete, beach balls were handed out to the participants. Jonah placed one of the colorful balls in Seth's hands. Seth began rubbing the ball and feeling the different sections.

"Each part of the ball is a different color," explained Jonah.

"What color am I feeling?" asked Seth.

"That section is orange," replied Jonah.

Seth's face brightened into a smile as he exclaimed, "ORANGE! I love orange!"

I watched as the boy silently rubbed orange. His smile never dimmed. He absolutely loved this color. I began wondering what I had been missing about orange all these years. Why was it not everyone's favorite color?

Just when I thought there could be no better color than orange, Seth slid his hand to another section. For the second time he asked Jonah, "What color am I feeling?"

Jonah replied, "Now you're touching yellow."

"Yellow!" repeated Seth with excitement. "I love yellow."

Watching Seth feel yellow was profound. His enthusiasm for orange was replaced with a reverence for yellow. His yellow was not part of a firework in the night or a daffodil gracing a garden. Seth's rendition of yellow was perfect. It made him feel respect, joy, and adoration all at the same time.

And then he stopped and said, "Hey, Jonah, it's too bad you're not blind so you could see what I'm seeing."

I thought about that statement many times during the remainder of that day. Seth didn't see with his eyes but with his heart. The colors he experienced were not limited by preconceived connections made through association. To him orange was more than the color of carrots and pumpkins. Yellow was not limited to dandelions and lemons. His blindness allowed him to experience colors without expectations or limits. Seth loved each color simply because it existed, and that gave it endless possibilities.

On the drive home I asked Jonah what he thought about Seth's comment.

"You never know what someone's experiencing. I thought I was helping him, but he ended up helping me," said Jonah.

"Did it change the way you see things?" I asked.

"It wasn't just the colors of the beach ball that he had deep feelings for, but it was for me too. The empathy he had for me was incredible," said Jonah. "I want to see people like Seth does. I'm going to make fewer judgments and have more appreciation for the people I meet."

A year later Jonah and his older brother, Jackson, came with me on a school visit to Thailand. On completion of our days at the school I had arranged for the three of us to spend a few days experiencing Thailand. On our first day of exploring, we headed to a busy shopping district.

I exchanged a sum of money from American dollars into Thai baht. I gave each boy some of the money. I told them to buy whatever they wanted but to manage their money because it needed to last for the entire trip.

As we made our way down a bustling street lined with shops, we entered store after store. I was looking for the perfect Buddha statue to remind me of peace and kindness. The boys wanted to find unique T-shirts that weren't available back home. When we were almost done with our shopping, Jonah still hadn't purchased a single item. In fact, he didn't even bother to enter many of the stores. I commented to Jackson that it was odd that his little brother hadn't seen one item he wanted.

"He's low on money," replied Jackson.

"How is that possible?" I asked. "He hasn't bought anything."

I left the store and found Jonah outside watching the assortment of bikes, cars, and tuk tuks weave themselves into the stream of noisy traffic that flowed down the street.

"Jackson said you have money trouble," I said.

"I don't have any problems with money," he replied.

"Do you still have the money I gave you?" I asked

"No," replied Jonah.

"Did you lose it?" I asked.

"I gave it to that lady," said Jonah.

"What lady?" I asked.

"The one holding the baby," answered Jonah.

"I didn't see a lady holding a baby," I replied.

"She was sitting in front of the first store we went into," said Jonah. "She was begging for money."

"How much of your money did you give her?" I asked.

"All of it," replied Jonah.

While I was looking for a statue of Buddha to remind me of peace and kindness, Jonah was experiencing peace and kindness. He saw with his heart while I was looking with consumer eyes for unnecessary souvenirs.

Years have passed since that trip. I don't know where my Buddha statue is, and Jackson no longer has the T-shirts he purchased. However, the feeling Jonah received from helping a young mother and her child will stay with him for his lifetime.

I think of the young boy who said, "Jonah, it's too bad you're not blind so you could see what I'm seeing." Jonah does see what Seth saw. He sees and loves others without expectations or limits. He appreciates the joy of helping and freely gives of his time and money. He lives a life of color.

gather

One snowflake's journey ended on a slight branch high in a tree. Soon other snowflakes began to gather around the tiny host. Each sparkling addition found its place with the group. Eventually, a pure white heart made of snow took shape. It all began with one seemingly insignificant snowflake. All gatherings can be traced back to one. The one who makes a positive suggestion. The one who invites a friend. The one who gives the first offering. Be the one.

Happiness gives you pleasure.
Joy gives you meaning.
Happiness makes you want more.
Joy makes you give more.
Happiness grows during fun times.
Joy sustains during tough times.
Happiness shows on your face.
Joy shows in your actions.
Happiness is situational.
Joy is long-lasting.
Happiness helps you have a good day.
Joy helps you live a good life.

The Money is Here

The moment I entered the library, I heard someone yell my name. An enthusiastic boy rushed up and introduced himself.

"My name is Ron and I'm your biggest fan," said the smiling eight-year-old.

I shook his hand and said, "I've always wanted to meet my biggest fan."

"I've read all your books. They're some of my favorites," said Ron, beaming.

I was doing a weeklong library tour in Clark County, Nevada. It had been a fun week with my daughter Annie and my son Boone traveling with me. Each day we would visit two libraries where I would do some storytelling and then have a book signing.

It was the last stop of the week when I met Ron. He stuck by my side as I was escorted through the main area of the library into a large room in the back where I was to do my presentation. As I began to unpack one of the boxes of books I had with me, Ron opened the other one and started to remove the books.

"Wait," I said. "I have a system."

"Me too," said Ron as he randomly scattered books around the table.

I introduced Ron to Annie and Boone and suggested he could sit by them during the storytelling.

"I'd rather not," said Ron as he followed me onto the small stage. "What stories are you going to tell?"

"*Look What the Cat Dragged In* and *Sir William the Worm*," I answered.

"Good picks," said Ron. "I know both of them."

When one of the librarians asked if I was ready to begin Ron said, "We're ready."

"Is this your son?" asked the librarian.

"This is Ron," I said. "He's here for the storytelling."

I was relieved when the librarian escorted Ron off the stage and found him a place in the audience. It was a large crowd, and they were enjoying my storytelling until Ron began shouting out what was going to happen next in the story right before I would say it. It wasn't fun for the audience, or me, but Ron was having a blast. At the conclusion of the program, Ron hurried to my side.

"I've been saving my money to buy some of your books," he announced.

"That's great," I replied.

"Not so great," said Ron. "I left the bag with the money at home. But don't worry. My mom went home to get it."

"Who is going to watch after you until she gets back?" I asked.

With a huge grin, he crowed, "You are. I'm your assistant."

There was a lengthy line of children eager to meet me and have me sign their books. As the first boy stepped up to the table, Ron wrenched the copy of *Sir William the Worm* out of his hands.

"I'll take it from here," said Ron, plopping the book in front of me and opening the book to the title page.

I sighed and said, "Ron, you should stay on this side of the table with me because I want to talk to these boys and girls while I sign their books."

"Gotcha," said Ron as he hurried around the table to stand at my side.

As I began to inscribe a message in the next book, Ron slowly read each word in a loud voice. When I made the hush sound, Ron announced that everyone needed to quiet down.

A young, red-haired girl placed a copy of *Look What the Cat Dragged In* on the table and smiled like an angel. I asked her name and began to write, "To Melanie, you make the world a happier place."

Ron read it and announced, "That's not true."

As the girl's smile disappeared, I turned to Ron and gave him a disapproving stare.

"I know her," he blurted in his own defense.

I suggested that Ron see if his mother was back with the money.

"Good idea," said Ron as he raced out of the room.

I was autographing a book for the last child in line when I realized that Ron had been gone for quite some time. It was at that moment that I heard him shouting my name at the top of his lungs.

"Gary Hogg! Gary Hogg! The money is here!" was echoing throughout the entire library.

Ron charged into the room and plopped a plastic bag containing the money on the table in front of me. I looked into the bag. It contained one wadded up dollar bill and some random coins.

"How many books can I get with this much money?" Ron asked while trying to catch his breath.

I looked up at Ron, my self-proclaimed biggest fan. This enthusiastic boy had made a mess of the book display, interrupted my storytelling, ignored my requests, and offended a sweet girl. And in his mind, he had done nothing but helped me from the minute we met.

I glanced back down at the bag of money and said, "It looks like you have just enough to buy all of your favorites."

Ron's face blossomed into a huge grin, and he exclaimed, "I knew it!"

He gathered up several of the books and placed them on the table for me to autograph. As I prepared to sign the first book, Ron insisted that I write, "To Ron, my very best friend in the world."

And so I did.

Ron was the main topic of discussion as we drove back to Utah that evening. Annie and Boone thought he was the funniest boy they had ever met.

“Were you like that when you were a boy?” asked Annie.

“Oh no, I was always the perfect gentleman,” I fibbed.

The truth is we are all like Ron. There are times that each of us shows up with less than is required to get what we need. Someone makes up the difference and we aren’t even aware they’ve done it. There are moments when our good intentions are more of a hindrance than a help, but out of kindness, no one draws attention to that fact. And on a different day, we need to be the one that picks up the slack or shows kindness to someone who has no idea they are testing our patience.

To believe you’ve earned everything you’ve ever gotten in life without anyone else’s help is shortsighted. Your life is impacted by the sacrifices made by many people, some whose names you’ll never know and others who are the first number on your speed dial.

celebrate

Your life is a celebration.
Like all humans, you're truly original,
often kind, occasionally quirky,
mostly brave, sometimes exceptional,
while other times flawed.
Your worst days don't define you
and your finest moments may go unnoticed.
Set your own course and let your heart guide you.

texture

Just as leaves give composition to bony branches of trees and clouds offer momentary structure to air, our relationships give our lives texture. We weave our way through life, embracing, twisting, mixing, meshing, and bonding with others in a perpetual motion that adds dimension and depth to our existence. The intertwining of life stories provides perspective that can be obtained no other way.

The Ten-Thousand-Mile Conversation

I was sitting in the bleachers watching a rodeo when the announcer reminded everyone of the 10K race that was to start at 6 a.m. the next morning. I looked over at my younger sister Sally and on an impulse said, "Do you want to run that race with me?"

"Of course, it'll be fun," was her reply. She was a veteran of many marathons and I had just turned forty and had never run more than a mile in my life. I had been suffering from anxiety over the breakup of my marriage and thought some exercise would be good for me.

The next morning, as the other runners were stretching, I looked down at my black, ankle-high socks and brown hiking shoes. It was obvious that I was the least qualified runner in the large group. Sally was running in place while telling me how much fun we were going to have.

The sheriff fired a shotgun into the air and the race was on. I slowly jogged down the gravel road. Sally stayed with me for a bit but when she saw how slow I was, she said that we'd meet up at the finish line.

My goal was to not walk a step of the race course. I was four miles into the race when Sally showed back up. She turned around and ran backward so we could talk face to face.

"You didn't have to wait for me," I said.

She laughed and said, "Oh, I already finished. I wanted to run back and cheer you on."

"You really are a great runner," I huffed as I plowed along.

"So are you," said Sally.

"Oh yeah, I'm a flash," I joked.

I could feel the blisters growing on my feet, a large one on the ball of my right foot and an equally painful one on my left heel. Finally, I crossed the finish line. I had run six miles in hiking shoes, while developing painful blisters. I was exhausted but also exhilarated. That morning, a runner was born.

Two days later, I bought my first pair of running shoes and shorts. I mapped out a five-mile loop and began to run every morning. It was the magic sauce I needed to deal with my anxious energy.

After a month of running, I came upon my neighbor Kim running the same loop. We were both slow go runners and kept each other company while we ran. It was fun to have someone to talk with while I counted off the miles.

The next morning, my phone rang at 6 a.m. It was Kim.

"Get out of bed, lazy bum," was her hello. "Put your shoes on and meet me in front of my house and we'll run."

And so, we ran.

The call came again the next morning, and again the following day. On the third morning, I met Kim and explained that I had reservations about running with her every day. I was a single dad. She was a happily married wife and mother.

"That's why I wasn't going to call you," said Kim. "But I prayed about it and God told me that you need a friend, and I am supposed to be that friend."

"You prayed about it?" I asked.

"I pray about everything," said Kim.

"What about Vern?" I asked. "What does he think?"

"I've talked it over with him and he's just glad that I'm exercising," was her reply.

"What about what people will say? There are some big gossips in the neighborhood," I added.

"God told me to be your friend. His opinion is more important than what some busybody might say," explained Kim. "Do you want to run?"

"Yes," I said.

"Then let's go," said Kim as she jogged down the road.

And that was how the ten-thousand-mile conversation began. God was right. I needed a friend like Kim. She was the kind of friend that would tell me when she thought I was wrong and always encouraged me to be my best. She offered much needed advice about raising my kids. She was a great storyteller and a patient listener. I have six wonderful sisters, but none of them live near me. Kim became my seventh sister, and she lived just across the street.

We ran through the summer and into the winter snow. It was a happy, healthy habit for both of us. We talked politics, sports, religion, literature, jokes, family, and every current hot topic of the day. Each day we just added to the conversation from the day before.

On an early morning run during the first year of running together, Kim looked at me and said, "I want you to speak at my funeral."

I stopped dead in my tracks and asked, "What's wrong with you?"

"Nothing," she said.

"No, really, what's wrong with you?" I repeated. "What kind of perfectly healthy person asks someone to talk at their funeral?"

"I do," said Kim. "Now tell me that you'll do it."

"No," I said. "I'll die before you, so I want you to talk at my funeral."

"I asked first," said Kim.

"But I'll die first," I said.

"I need you to tell me that you'll speak at my funeral," said Kim.

"Who else have you asked?" I asked.

"No one," said Kim. "That would be weird."

"You're right," I said. "This entire conversation is weird."

"Tell me that you'll do it," insisted Kim.

"OK, I'll speak at your funeral," I said. "Are you happy now?"

"It better be a really good talk," said Kim.

"This conversation is over," I said and sprinted down the dirt road.

During a springtime run, Kim asked, "Have you ever noticed how attractive Vern's legs are?"

"No, I don't spend much time looking at other men's legs," I responded.

"Next time you see him in shorts, look at his calves. They are magnificent," she said.

"No, thank you," I replied.

"You know *Pride and Prejudice* is my favorite book," said Kim. "My dream is for Vern to dress up like Mr. Darcy. He'd wear a white lacey shirt, long tail jacket, black pants that end at the knee, tight white socks that show off his masculine calves, topped off with a top hat. Can't you just picture it?"

I laughed aloud and said, "Nope, but keep dreaming."

And with a swoon in her voice, she sang, "Vern is my Mr. Darcy. He is my true love."

Our running slowed down one year as Kim was pregnant with a baby boy. Adam was stillborn, and it devastated Kim's entire family. I'd never seen Kim so sad. I didn't think we would ever run together again. After several months, I received a phone call.

"Can we run?" asked Kim.

"When?" I asked.

"Now," she said.

I met her in front of her house. We ran in silence. Her heart was mending, and she didn't need advice. She needed support.

"Thank you," said Kim at the conclusion of our run.

"You're welcome," I replied.

"Tomorrow?" she asked.

"Yes," I replied.

After twelve years of running, I made the big announcement. "Kim, we have run over ten thousand miles."

"Hmm," said Kim, unimpressed. "All those miles and we didn't get very far from home."

It was less than a year later when Kim ended our daily runs. She was crying as she explained that she had prayed about it.

"Are you sure?" I asked.

"No, but God is," was her reply.

I kept running, but I missed my little sister Kim. I often found myself wanting to tell her a story or needing some of her advice. I saw her at church, and we'd catch up on the phone, but it wasn't the same. There is something about talking while moving that makes a conversation more meaningful.

The call came late one afternoon a year later. It was Kim, and I knew something was wrong the second I answered the phone.

"What's the matter?" I asked.

"Do you remember that I told you I've felt a bit off lately?" she asked.

"Yes," I said as a feeling of dread filled my heart.

"I had some tests. I have ovarian cancer and it is very bad," said Kim.

"I'm coming right over," I said, hanging up the phone and heading to Kim's house.

Kim explained the situation and gave me details about her prognosis. The oncologist wanted to be aggressive, utilizing surgery and chemotherapy to fight the cancer. Even with using every available treatment, she felt that Kim would have a limited lifespan. It was the hardest I have ever cried in my life.

"She could be wrong," I said. "You could receive a miracle."

"I'm praying for one," said Kim. "Whenever the end comes, remember you promised to speak at my funeral."

Kim fought the cancer with all her energy and faith. She would seem to be much better, but then inevitably a setback would come. Through it all she never lost her sense of humor or her courage.

It was three years into Kim's battle that I received a call from her. She sounded upbeat and much stronger.

"Hey, I've been walking to build up my stamina. I'm calling to see if you want to do our loop one more time. I can't run, but I think I can walk the entire five miles," she explained.

I was thrilled.

"You name the day and time and I'll be there," I said.

It was a beautiful day in August when we took the last lap. We had fun telling stories, just like old times. We were on the last mile of a conversation that covered more than ten thousand miles when Kim slowed our already slow walk to a snail's pace.

"I don't have much time left," she said.

I remained silent.

"I'm not scared, and I know Vern and the kids are going to be all right. I've prayed about it," she said.

Then, after a long pause, she continued, "I just want my life to have mattered."

I didn't speak. I knew that Kim wasn't looking for validation from me. Faith, family, friendship, sense of humor, loyalty, honesty, kindness, generosity, and love are the only things that really do matter in life. Kim was the perfect example of all those qualities.

Three months later, I was doing school visits in the panhandle of Texas when I received a call from Kim's daughter, Kali. I already knew what the call was about before Kali said a word. We talked for a bit, and then she asked if I would speak at her mother's funeral.

"It will be an honor," I said.

It was the biggest funeral I have ever attended. The church's chapel and accompanying gym were overflowing. It was a celebration of a life that mattered. It wasn't difficult to decide what to say during my remarks. Kim asked me to speak at her funeral and then spent thousands of miles telling me the stories that would be the foundation of that talk. They were stories of friendship, faith, and family. They were love stories about an understanding husband who was Kim's Mr. Darcy and her brilliant children, whom she adored.

Every run has a beginning, a point in time when you decide to take the first step. I wore black socks and brown shoes on the first official run of my life. I wasn't prepared or in shape for it. I thought I needed exercise, but God knew I needed a friend.

grit

Hope is the feeling that today's trials don't have to be tomorrow's ordeals. Determination is the resolve to find a better way. Grit is the tough stuff that results from combining the ambition of hope with the courage of determination. Grit is the agent of change that teaches perseverance. It makes hard things doable. Grit provides the humility, appreciation, and strength to realize your best self. When in doubt, use your grit.

live

Each beat of your heart adds to the rhythms and patterns of our living world. Your piece in the puzzle of life is not trivial or exclusive. You are both a receiver and contributor to the expanse of nature. Make your minutes on earth matter. Accept your challenge. Awaken your courage. Share your ideas. Offer your help. Be part of a solution. Find joy. Give respect. Live a good life.

Allergic to Pork

During my twenties, Will Rogers was my hero. He was a writer, cowboy, and entertainer who died in 1939. For a time, he was the most popular and highest paid actor in Hollywood. What drew me to Will Rogers was not his fame, but his love for people. His most famous quote was, "I never met a man I didn't like."

We had just set up camp on the edge of Redfish Lake in the Sawtooth Mountains of Idaho when TJ coasted into our campsite on his cousin's bike. The first thing I noticed about him was that he never stopped smiling. The second thing I noticed was that this happy eight-year-old boy was missing his right foot.

It was a tradition for TJ's family, including his grandpa, grandma, uncles, aunts, and all the cousins to spend a week at Redfish Lake each year. When we arrived, TJ was eager to meet the new neighbors.

TJ reminded me of a young Will Rogers. He was funny, sincere, smart, and there was no doubt he liked you before he met you. When he caught my wife, Emily, looking at his prosthesis, he was completely at ease relating the story of the operation that removed his foot when he was just one year old. He showed us his prosthesis and explained how his leg slides into the sleeve which has the foot attached at the base.

In a matter of minutes, TJ had endeared himself to our entire group. When he climbed on his cousin's bike to leave, Emily invited him to come back to our campfire that evening.

We were toasting marshmallows over the fire when TJ walked back into our camp. I looked up and asked, "TJ, can I toast you a marshmallow?"

"No, thanks," he called out. "I'm allergic to pork."

Confused by his response, I repeated my question, "Do you want me to toast you a marshmallow?"

"I heard you the first time," said TJ. "I'm allergic to pork."

"I'm not asking if you want a hot dog," I insisted. "I'm toasting marshmallows."

"Marshmallows have gelatin in them," explained TJ. "They use pork to make it. Look it up sometime."

And then his grin grew a bit bigger, and he asked, "Do you want to hear the story about how we found out I was allergic to pork? I warn you it involves throw-up."

Of course, we wanted to hear the story. TJ had a captive audience, and he was an expert storyteller.

"It all started in this very campground, in the exact campsite you are in," said TJ. "I was barely three years old, and my parents kept feeding me hot dogs and marshmallows. We were camping. That's what you eat. I gobbled them down and then later I'd throw up. It was gross. I just couldn't stop throwing up. There was throw-up everywhere."

"We got the throw-up part," I said, trying to move the story along.

"Right," said TJ. "Finally, after my parents couldn't handle the throw-up anymore, they took me to a doctor. The doctor figured out I was allergic to pork. Now I find out if something contains pork before I eat it. You won't believe all the things that have pig in them. It's a lot."

While I added a log to the fire, my sister Verda asked TJ to tell us another story.

"There's the mystery of the missing foot, but you probably don't want to hear that one," said TJ.

"Yes, we do," said Emily.

TJ smiled and began, "Before I go to bed, I take off my foot and leave it next to my bed. The first thing I do in the morning is put it back on. But one day when I woke up, my foot had disappeared."

"Where did it go?" asked Emily.

"That was the big mystery," said TJ. "Who would take a kid's foot while he's sleeping?"

"That's horrible," said Verda.

"I know," said TJ. "It's my foot."

"How did you find it?" asked Emily.

"I hopped around on one leg until I found the thief," said TJ.

"Who was it?" I asked.

"My little brother," said TJ, grinning. "He was using it as a weapon."

A picture of a six-year-old beating someone with his brother's artificial foot popped into my mind as I asked, "Who did he hit with it?"

"No one," said TJ. "He was playing army with his friends, and my foot was his pretend gun."

"Did you get mad at him?" asked Emily.

"Naw, he's my brother and it made him happy," said TJ. "I like it when he's happy."

"That's a grownup way to look at it. Are you sure you're only eight-years-old?" I asked.

"I'm going into third grade," said TJ.

"Well then, that it explains it," I said with a laugh.

"Do you like school?" asked Verda.

"PE is sometimes hard. When they play dodgeball, I have to sit out," said TJ.

"That must make you feel bad," said Emily.

"No, I love watching my friends have fun. It makes me happy," said TJ.

TJ loved listening to stories as much as telling them. We were kindred spirits in that department. We all took turns swapping stories around the campfire for the rest of the evening. As the coals in the firepit began to lose their glow, TJ told one last story.

"There was a girl in Utah who was going to have one of her legs amputated. When I heard about her, I knew I had to see her. I bugged my parents to take me to her house when we were on a trip to Utah," explained TJ.

"What did you do when you met her?" I asked.

"I ran around her yard so she could watch me. I wanted her to know that she would still be able to run when she got her prosthesis. And then I sat down next to her," said TJ.

"What did you say to her?" I asked.

"Nothing," said TJ. "I just wanted her to know she wasn't alone."

At eight years old, TJ understood two of life's most valuable lessons. Kindness comes from patience, and courage comes from sharing.

On the last day of our camping trip, TJ met us early in the morning to go on a short hike. As we walked, Emily said to TJ, "You are going to grow up to be a great man. I think you may become the president or a prophet."

"Or a comedian," I added. "You're a great storyteller."

We ended up at the tiny store at the north end of the lake. While Emily shopped for a sweatshirt, I offered to buy TJ a present.

"We could get matching hats," I offered.

"I like my old one," said TJ.

"What about a new T-shirt?" I asked.

"I have plenty of clothes," he replied.

"Do you want some candy?" I asked.

"You would not believe how much candy my grandma has at her camp," said TJ.

"I'd like to give you something for being so nice to us this week," I said.

"I don't want anything. I just like being with you guys. It makes me happy," said TJ, smiling.

We took a family picture on the pier before heading back to camp. TJ offered to be the photographer. As he told us to smile, I couldn't help but notice the smile on his face. It made me think of when he coasted into our camp on his cousin's bike and began telling stories. They were tales of dangerous marshmallows, brotherly love, friendship, and kindness.

I was reminded of another one of Will Rogers' famous quotes, "The worst thing that happens to you may be the best thing for you if you don't let it get the best of you."

Missing a foot does not get the best of TJ. He offers his best to the people he meets. Going through life with an artificial foot is not an excuse for sympathy for him. It's a way to make new friends. And friends are what make him happy.

welcome

The sky is the great accepter. It lets the sun set and the clouds play. It holds countless stars and a child's kite. The sky gives us air, moisture, and inspiration. It sets the ultimate example of how to invite, recieve, and provide. The human spirit is made of the same endless energy. You were created to welcome and bless, to give and accept. This intrinsic ability can guide you. It can be your North Star, a reassuring standard in the constellation of your life.

HUMBLE

Humility gives you kindness.
Kindness gives you patience.
Patience gives you understanding.
Understanding gives you wisdom.
Wisdom gives you gratitude.
Gratitude gives you humility.
And so it goes . . .

An Introduction to Grace

As a boy, I attended Miller Elementary School on Normal Avenue in Burley, Idaho. There were lots of ways to get hurt at Miller Elementary in the late 1960s. The blacktop playground was spacious and included lots of old-school dangers. As students we were always testing the limits.

The swings had long chains and we would swing as high as possible and then rocket out of the seat to see who could fly the farthest. The huge metal monkey bars were famous for breaking arms. My favorite was the towering metal slide. During freezing winter days, we'd take crayons, wax the bottom of our leather-soled shoes, and zoom down the frozen metal in a crouching position. The slide spilled out onto an icy track that we made by packing snow and covering it with water that quickly turned to ice. There were some spectacular crashes.

As with all schools, there were some kids that came to Miller Elementary already hurting. Their lack of focus had nothing to do with what was going on at school. Acting out was not an act of rebellion. Unkind words came easy to them because that was the language that was spoken in their homes.

Donna came to fifth grade with some baggage but, like most of my classmates, I didn't know anything about any of her personal struggles. All I knew was that she fluctuated from being wiggly and giggly to being mad at the whole world and everyone in it. She was often alone at recess and was always picked last when teams were chosen.

Mrs. Burnsides was my fifth grade teacher. She loved games and would incorporate them into our learning whenever she could. We regularly played *Seven Up*, *Hot Potato*, and *Time Bomb*. I'll never forget the day she carried a piñata into our room. I didn't know what it was until Brian whispered to me that the funny-looking donkey was full of candy.

"Someone's going to bust it open, and we get the sweet stuff," said my best friend.

Mrs. Burnsides let the suspense grow until we returned from morning recess. We entered our second-story classroom to find our desks and chairs had all been pushed back. The brightly colored donkey was hanging from a small rope that was attached to the ceiling in the middle of the room.

It didn't take long for us to form a circle around the doomed donkey. We all wanted to be first to have a crack at destroying the colorful piñata. To everyone's surprise, Mrs. Burnsides selected Donna.

"Why Donna?" whined several of my classmates.

"Because I said so," was the only response offered by our teacher.

Donna stepped forward amid a grumbling of protests. The girl who never got to go first was finally getting her chance, and no one was happy for her. I could see the disappointment on her face.

Mrs. Burnsides handed a red bandana to Donna and asked her to tie it around her head to cover her eyes. She then took Donna by the shoulders and spun her in a circle. Finally, our teacher placed a long broomstick into Donna's hands.

We all knew Donna was strong enough to crush the donkey with one mighty crash, so we were ready to dash in for the candy that was about to rain down.

Before our beloved teacher could get out of the way, Donna took the first big swing with the broom handle. The wooden rod missed the donkey by a mile but hit Mrs. Burnsides. We all gasped. And then Donna took another swing and whacked our teacher a second time.

"Donna can see what she's doing," yelled one of the girls. "She's peeking out from under the bandana."

Donna dropped the broom handle and ripped the bandana away from her eyes. All the air was sucked out of the room as we held our breath, waiting to see what Mrs. Burnsides was going to do.

Donna stood her ground while Mrs. Burnsides picked up the broom handle. Our teacher took a deep breath and collected her thoughts. She then walked over to Donna. She took the bandana and tied it around Donna's head again, covering her eyes. Mrs. Burnsides then placed the broom handle back in Donna's hands.

"This time, no swinging until I give you the signal," said Mrs. Burnsides in a calm, even voice.

Donna tried again but never broke the piñata. Neither did the next three kids. Finally, one of the boys got a lucky swing and candy exploded onto the floor of our room.

I don't remember getting any of that candy. I was still trying to process what I had seen and felt. I didn't know if Donna had hit Mrs. Burnsides on purpose or by accident. But either way, my teacher had done something extraordinary. That morning at Miller Elementary was the first time I had ever witnessed true grace. A second chance was extended. Hurtful words were withheld. Patience was given to someone who hadn't earned it. Mrs. Burnsides used kindness to extend hope for a young girl who truly needed it.

Years later, I realized that Mrs. Burnsides knew some of the reasons why Donna acted the way she did in class. She understood the source of some of the disappointments and frustrations that were a daily part of Donna's life. What had started out as a fun game with a piñata donkey turned into an invaluable life lesson.

Knowing why a person acts the way he or she does can make a significant difference in how we interact. However, we rarely have this valuable insight. The judgments we make are often based on limited information and are often misguided.

Life is a dangerous playground. There are always people who will test our limits. While I may not know the *why* behind someone else's actions, I can always understand the *why* behind my responses. Like Mrs. Burnsides, I can extend grace because that's the kind of person I choose to be. The most important *why* is always answered within your own heart.

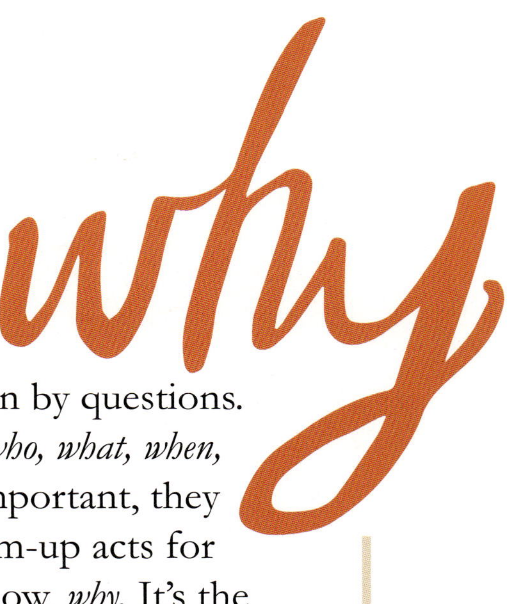

Curiosity is driven by questions. Although *how, who, what, when,* and *where* are important, they are merely warm-up acts for the star of the show, *why.* It's the query that solves crimes and leads to breakthroughs and discoveries. This three-letter word has the power to change your life. When you understand *why,* you will be able to forgive *who*, not worry about *when*, choose the correct *what*, figure out *where* and have faith in *how.*

Care

A million-year-old rock is nestled in a bed of morning snow. Life is a manifestation of contrasts, ancient and new, fragile and solid, temporary and permanent. Each texture and timeline offers context and essence. No two opposites affect our hearts more than apathy and empathy. The simple act of caring can offer understanding when indifference could rule the day. Caring nurtures kindness and fends off prejudice. It is the softening balm for a hard heart. It is the precursor to love.

You Have a Monkey in Your Car

Every child has a dream. When my son Boone was ten years old, he was wild about monkeys. His dream was to have a monkey for a best friend. He was convinced they were smarter, funnier, and kinder than humans.

During a speaking tour in Seattle, Washington, I bought Boone a rust-colored, tie-dyed T-shirt with the face of a monkey screen printed on the front. Once he slid the T-shirt over his head, it was the only shirt he wanted to wear.

It wasn't just me; Boone's brothers and sister were always on the lookout for monkey gifts for their little brother. We weren't monkey superfans, but we loved Boone and were happy to support him in his monkey mania.

The year Boone turned eleven, I rented a condominium in Mexico for a family vacation. I had visited the Riviera Maya district several times in past years and always saw spider monkeys living in the surrounding jungle. Naturally, Boone was overjoyed when I told him that it was going to be his chance to come face-to-face with a monkey.

From the moment we arrived in Mexico, Boone was on the lookout for a monkey. The first monkey encounter came during our second day in

Mexico. We were in one of the wildest parts of the country, the shopping district of Playa del Carmen.

A man had a tired-looking spider monkey sitting on his shoulder. For a fee, you could have your picture taken with the monkey. As we approached the man and the monkey, Boone held out his hand, and the scrawny spider monkey gave him a lackluster high five.

"Can I hold him?" asked Boone.

I pulled some pesos out of my pocket and gave them to the man. He placed the monkey on Boone's shoulders.

"He likes me," said Boone, grinning.

Boone's older brother, Jackson, laughed and said, "He likes you so much, he just gave you a present."

"Ewww," said Annie. "The monkey just went number two on Boone."

"Does that cost extra?" joked Jonah.

The monkey held out his skinny arms and the man picked him up. They walked away, leaving us to clean up the mess.

The other kids thought it was hilarious and were eager to razz their little brother. Boone managed the situation with his remarkable sense of humor. He met their jokes with jokes of his own. It was our first funny family story of the trip.

The next day I had a day trip planned to visit the Mayan ruins in Tulum. Our group increased by three when I invited a neighbor from Utah and her two daughters to join us.

"How are eight people going to fit into a tiny car?" asked Jackson.

"It will be a squeeze, but we can do it," I replied.

It took three tries, but we finally got everyone into our little rental car.

"That was easy," I joked as I started the car.

"You don't have two people sitting on you and another person's armpit in your face," replied Jackson.

We spent most of the morning and part of the afternoon walking around what was left of an ancient civilization that overlooked the Caribbean Sea.

"What do you think of the ruins?" I asked.

"They're ruined," said Jackson in a bored voice. "Let's get out of here."

We crammed into our tiny rental car and headed back to our condominium. The kids were clearly disappointed that we had spent a good portion of the day staring at rock structures.

"That was boring," said Jonah.

The trip was not off to the best start. I needed some reinforcements, and I knew just where to find them. I took a hard left turn and drove down a dusty dirt road.

"This isn't the way to the condo," protested Jackson. "Where are we going?"

"It's crowded in here," grumbled Jonah.

"We're going to hang out with some wild monkeys," I announced.

"Monkeys!" shouted Boone as he stretched his neck to look out the windshield.

"I happen to know that spider monkeys live in these trees," I bragged.

The kids were on high alert as I slowed the car so we could search the branches for long-legged spider monkeys. We drove for over two miles without seeing so much as the tip of a monkey's tail.

"Where are all the monkeys?" asked Boone, his voice dripping with disappointment.

"Be patient," I said. "They're just being shy today."

After another mile, Jonah said, "Nice try, Dad, but let's go back to the condo."

I was about to do a U-turn when my daughter Annie, who was sitting in the shotgun seat, yelled, "There's a monkey on the road."

I hit the brakes hard and slid to a stop. She was right. Standing in the middle of the road was a long-tailed spider monkey. Everyone started talking at once.

"I get to hold him first," shouted Boone.

"You can't hold this one," I said, turning off the car. "This is a wild monkey who lives in the jungle. If we're quiet, we can sneak up close enough to get a picture."

That's when the monkey started running toward our car.

"Oh, yeah, here he comes," said Boone with excitement.

The monkey climbed onto the hood of the car and peered at us through the windshield. His puny monkey knuckles rapped on the glass.

"He wants to be our friend," said Boone.

Annie unrolled her window a couple of inches, and the monkey stuck its bony finger through the open gap in the window and wiggled it like a worm on a hook. Annie took the bait. She gently petted the pad of the monkey's middle finger and said, "Oh, Dad, it feels just like velvet."

I had to get a picture of this. I grabbed my camera and got out of the car. When I got out, I left the car door open. Like a hungry kid heading for a hot breakfast, the monkey scurried across the top of the car and jumped through the open door.

The car erupted into screams. It was monkey mayhem as the monkey climbed around on people's heads and slapped them in their faces.

The other three doors flew open, and, like crazy clowns at a circus, everyone jumped out of the tiny car. Now we were in the jungle, and the monkey had full control of our car. He started off by searching under the seats. He then rummaged through Annie's backpack.

When he climbed on the steering wheel, Jonah said, "If he gets the car started and drives off, we're in trouble."

After several minutes of monkey business, Jackson suggested we go back to the condominium.

"OK, I'll get the monkey out of the car," I announced.

I slid into the driver's seat and tried to shoo the monkey out the passenger's door. When that failed, I tried to get hold of one of his arms to pull him out of the car. This caused the monkey to screech and try to bite me. My heart pounded as I clambered back out of the car.

I did what most good dads would do. I turned to my oldest son and said, "Jackson, you get the monkey out of the car."

"No problem," he said. He squared his broad shoulders and entered the car with authority.

Fifteen seconds later, he floundered out of the car, yelling, "That monkey is a maniac."

I turned to my next son, Jonah, and issued the same challenge.

"Get the monkey out of the car."

Jonah is just the opposite of Jackson. He's a wiry guy and loves to show up his older brother.

"I'm all over this," said Jonah.

With the monkey in the front passenger seat, Jonah decided he would try an assault from the rear. Like a ninja, he slid into the backseat without the monkey noticing. His plan was to startle the monkey and scare it out of the open door.

Jonah began screaming as he hurled himself over the seat. Instead of leaving the car, the monkey jumped into the backseat. Jonah tried again and launched himself into the backseat. The monkey scrambled back into the front seat. Jonah was warming up for a third try when the monkey beat him to the punch.

The monkey came flying over the seat and landed right in front of my son. Jonah blasted out of the car screaming, "Dad, that monkey just tried to kill me!"

I turned to Boone, and before I could speak, Boone shook his head and said, "No way."

"I thought you loved monkeys," I said.

"Not that one," said Boone.

I was trying to think of a new plan when I noticed a park ranger coming up the road, heading straight for us. He walked right up to the car and looked through the windshield at the monkey.

"You've got a monkey in your car," said the ranger.

"Yeah, I noticed," I replied.

The ranger then scolded me right in front of my kids.

"You are not supposed to let a monkey get in your car," he said.

I quickly apologized. "I'm sorry, but I can't get him out. Will you help me?"

The ranger let out a heavy sigh and said, "OK, I'll get the monkey out of your car."

We watched as the ranger slid into the driver's seat and stared at the monkey. Suddenly, as loud as he could, he started screaming at the monkey.

The monkey stared back at the ranger, and as loud as he could he began screeching at the ranger.

That is when I noticed the ranger's right hand. It was slowly moving toward the monkey. The screaming was a distraction. Suddenly, as quick as a snake strikes, the ranger had the monkey's noodle-like tail in his grip.

The ranger stepped out of the car, dragging the monkey by its tail. The spider monkey was furious. He scrambled up a tree and began breaking off sticks and leaves and throwing them at us.

"That is a crazy monkey," I said to the ranger.

"I know this monkey," said the ranger. "Some time ago, a family came into the jungle and gave this monkey some candy. That was a very bad idea. Ever since that day, this monkey is not afraid of humans and thinks they all have candy."

"That must have been what he was looking for when he searched the car," I said.

"If you have some candy, I will use it to bring him back out of the tree and you can get a picture of him," said the ranger.

I turned to the kids and asked, "Do we have any candy?"

"No, Dad, you ate it all," said Jonah.

That's when I remembered a bottle of Sprite I had in the trunk. I quickly retrieved it and asked the ranger if it would do the trick.

The ranger twisted the bright green cap and poured a tiny bit of Sprite into the bottle cap. The monkey came scrambling out of the tree. He perched himself on the hood of the car and begged for a sip of the sparkling soda. We watched as the ranger held the cap for the monkey to lap up the Sprite. The ranger said that the kids could each have a turn holding the cap so that I could get a picture of them with the monkey.

"Who wants to go first?" asked the ranger.

We all looked at Boone. This was his big moment, and we were excited for him. Boone was beaming as he watched the monkey drink the soda. He was making a new friend the same way we all make new friends, by sharing.

One by one, we all took turns holding the bottle cap. I got to go last. I will always remember how tight that monkey gripped my finger as he took a sip of soda. I felt a real connection. Not with the monkey, but with my son Boone. I'm sure my other kids felt it too. Boone's love for monkeys made the experience much more meaningful for all of us.

There wasn't any complaining as we piled into the rental car for the third time that day. Bad moods were replaced with laughter as we took turns telling our favorite parts of the monkey encounter.

Boone's monkey shirt eventually came apart at the seams and over time he lost his desire to have a monkey for a best friend. His love of monkeys was replaced with a passion for music. Whether it's monkeys or music, as a family, we support him with all our hearts. Standing on common ground with loved ones is what makes families strong. Retelling the funny and tender stories of our lives is what keeps families connected.

BLOOM

Yarrow plants have tiny flowers that cluster together giving the appearance of one larger blossom. The beauty of each tiny bloom is multiplied by the cooperation of its fellow delicate companions. Each insignificant petal is important to the propagation of this perennial herb. Like the precious petals of the yarrow your heart's potential is amplified when you are deeply connected with those in your life circles. You become smarter, kinder, more engaging as you contribute to the well-being of those around you.

laugh

Bruises, fractures, sprains, and strains both physical and emotional come at unpredictable times. A healthy sense of humor offers a counterweight to the heaviness of stress and tension that accompanies an injury to the heart or body. Laughter is the universal language. It lightens loads and lifts spirits. It provides distraction and introduces new perspectives. Humor can help your heart grow even when you feel like shrinking.

The Kindest Boy

There's nothing quite as intriguing as a treasure chest. I was a teenager when Grandma Hogg took me into her spare bedroom and pulled out a small wooden box.

"What's inside?" I asked.

"Treasures," answered Grandma.

My grandmother opened the box and took the items out one at a time. With each treasure, Grandma told me the story that bound that item to her heart.

Just like Grandma Hogg, I have a treasure chest in my office. Each item holds value because of the person and story attached to it. One of those treasures is a beautiful white, brown, and sky blue afghan. It was given to me by one of the kindest people I have ever met.

My friendship with Keygan began with the opening of a door. I was eating lunch with Jan Green in her office at Stalker Elementary School when an energetic fifth grader suddenly stepped into the room. Keygan was a small boy with a big personality.

The school was in the middle of a Krispy Kreme doughnut fundraiser, and Keygan was determined to outraise all the other students. He was hitting up everyone he could find to buy doughnuts.

Keygan hurried over to Jan with the sign-up sheet. She joked around with him before getting out her checkbook and buying a dozen doughnuts. Keygan then turned his attention to me. He explained that I would pay for the doughnuts today and in two weeks they would be delivered to the school.

"I would love to buy some doughnuts, but there is a problem. When the Krispy Kremes are delivered, I won't be around to eat them," I explained.

Keygan's smile faded.

"But if I could find someone who would volunteer to eat the doughnuts for me, I'd gladly buy a dozen," I continued.

Keygan's hand shot into the air. Like a perfect student, he waited for me to call on him.

When I did, he announced, "I volunteer to eat the doughnuts for you."

"Perfect," I said.

As I pulled out my wallet, Keygan added, "If you bought two dozen doughnuts, I could share with my friends."

Everyone in the room laughed and I paid for two dozen doughnuts. I gave Keygan the money and he hurried out of the room to find his next customer.

My last writing workshop of the day was with the fifth graders. It was held in the gymnasium to accommodate all the classes at the same time. Keygan and his aide were the first ones to arrive. They sat down in two chairs next to the wall. I made my way over to visit with Keygan before the workshop began.

"Do you ever give a free book to a really kind boy?" he asked.

"Oh, yes," I said. "I would today if I could find a really kind boy."

Keygan's face brightened into a smile as his hand shot in the air. He patiently waited for me to call on him, and when I did, he announced, "I'm a really kind boy."

"Well, that works out great," I said. "Let's pick out a book for you."

He chose *Beware of the Cheese Princess*, and I autographed it with a personalized message just for him.

It was obvious that Keygan had faced more than his share of challenges in his young life. I didn't know how many difficulties he had experienced until I visited with Jan at the end of the school day.

She explained that this incredible boy was born with Nager syndrome. This unfortunate condition comes with a myriad of health challenges: underdeveloped bones, breathing difficulties, hearing loss, and many other problems and concerns.

On top of all his health struggles, Keygan had the additional challenge of having been placed in the foster care system at an early age. He had had eight different foster families before the Wright family adopted him.

Several years later, I was autographing books during a school visit in eastern Idaho when a smiling teacher introduced herself as Keygan's sister. I was eager to hear what was going on in the life of this remarkable young man.

"He's a teenager now," said Shantel as she showed me pictures of Keygan on her phone. His smile was brighter than ever. She then scrolled through pictures of children wrapped in beautifully crocheted blankets.

"Keygan made all these blankets," she explained. "He had spent so much time at Primary Children's Hospital in Salt Lake City that he wanted to find a way to help the children that are receiving care there. So, he taught himself to crochet by watching YouTube videos. He uses all his money and most of his free time to make these blankets."

I got Keygan's address from Shantel and wrote him a letter. As soon as he received the letter, he tracked down my phone number and a text message from him soon arrived.

Since then, we have kept our friendship going through frequent text message conversations. It is a relationship that I treasure. His sense of humor and positive personality are always a source of inspiration for me.

Keygan has had sixty-seven surgeries, including reconstructive surgeries on his face, ankle, elbows, fingers, and wrists. He has also undergone multiple operations on his ears and eyes. His life has been one extensive list of challenges. Yet on top of that mountain of problems and worries, Keygan stands tall, raising his hand, and declaring, "I am a really kind boy."

When the pandemic began running rampant through the world, I immediately became worried about Keygan. I texted him and asked if he was keeping himself safe. This is his return text.

We are prepared for these days ahead.
I'm making something for you!!!
Hope you are excited.

Two weeks later, a package arrived for me. I was surprised and excited to pull out a beautiful white, brown, and sky blue afghan. It was crocheted with love by one of the most exceptional humans I have ever met. It is bound to my heart with friendship and kept safe in a wooden treasure chest.

Moss was the first land plant on earth. For hundreds of millions of years, it has graced the planet with its vibrant green hues. This tenacious plant can flourish on stone or wood or supply a rich carpet for the forest's floor. The ability to thrive with whatever life allows is key to happiness. You can wait for a better situation, an easier starting point, a guarantee of success, or like the humble moss you can thrive where you are with what you have.

appreciate

The two most important words in any language are *thank you*. Giving thanks is the code that acknowledges that you are a part of something intricate and interdependent. It strengthens your bonds with those you love and allows you to contribute to the well-being of a stranger. Gratitude is the prerequisite for humility and opens the door for happiness.

How to Change a Life

I can't remember my first grade teacher's name. What I can remember is that she was stern and carried a ruler. If you got out of line, this grouchy woman would motion for you to stick your hands out, palms up. She would then smack each hand with the ruler.

I had made up a ridiculously dumb joke and could not wait to share it with my favorite classmate, Karen Clark. We were lined up to go to lunch when I began to tell the joke. Our teacher heard me and turned toward me with the ruler in hand. I knew what was coming and stuck my hands out. As my teacher raised the ruler, I blurted out, "Wait, don't you want to hear the joke first?"

"No," she snapped as the ruler smacked my six-year-old hand.

I didn't mind the sting of the ruler. What bothered me was that she wouldn't even take the time to listen to the joke. I decided that day that teachers had no idea what was funny.

That all changed when I entered the fourth grade. The week before school was to start, I was riding Snoopy, a new horse my dad had purchased. When I kicked him into a run, he dropped his head and started bucking. He launched me into the air, and I came down headfirst. I ended up with a broken right arm. I saw this as my lucky break. How could I be expected to start school with my arm in a full cast? I'm right-handed, which meant I couldn't write.

My mother saw things differently. She escorted me to Miller Elementary on the first day of school so she could meet my teacher and make sure she understood that I was not to use my broken wing as an excuse to get out of any schoolwork.

Susan Bingham was my new teacher's name. She was the youngest teacher I had ever seen. Most of the teachers at Miller Elementary were well into their teaching careers. Miss Bingham looked more like an older sister than a mom or grandma.

She had red hair and kind eyes and wore modern clothes. And, best of all, she giggled. Laughter has always been my favorite language, and my new teacher was fluent. When I discovered that I could make her laugh out loud, I was smitten.

I loved school because I loved making her laugh. My comedy routines got louder and more involved as the year progressed. I regularly disrupted class with my crazy ideas.

The invitation came during the first part of November. "I need to see you after school today," said Miss Bingham.

I only lived a block from Miller Elementary, so I ran straight home after school and informed my mother. She was instantly concerned.

"What have you done?" she asked.

"Nothing," I answered.

"Did she say she wanted me to come too?" asked Mom.

"No, she just needs to see me," I said.

When I got back to Miller Elementary School, the kids were all gone. I had never been in the halls when they were so quiet. I opened our classroom door and spotted Miss Bingham at her desk, grading papers. Her face brightened into a smile, and she quickly invited me over.

"I was thinking about you last night," she said.

"What did you think?" I asked.

"I thought you've been spending more time working on jokes than doing your schoolwork," said Miss Bingham.

"I thought you liked my jokes," I said.

"I do," said my teacher as the smile came back to her face. "You are very funny. That's why I asked you to come in today. I think you should start writing your ideas into stories instead of acting them out in class. I have a feeling that someday those stories will become books. Those books are going to sell all over the world. Last night I decided that I wanted to be the first person in the universe to get your autograph."

"You want my autograph?" I asked suspiciously.

She pulled a picture out of the top drawer of her desk and placed it in front of me. It was a full page advertisement for Planters Peanuts. Printed above Mr. Peanut were the words, *I'm a nut!*

"Sign it to Miss Bingham, please," she said.

Susan Bingham was suddenly one of the smartest people I had ever met. Not because she thought I was funny but because she knew I was funny for a reason. That information made all the difference.

I can't remember what I wrote besides my name, but I can remember how I felt. It was the feeling that I had found a place where I belonged. My funny ideas and silly personality were needed in the world. There were stories that I was going to write that no other person who ever lived would write. At nine years old, I realized that I didn't have to be like anyone else in this world.

Like all great teachers, Miss Bingham recognized the best in me. She saw me as a creative person when she could have viewed me as a troublemaker. She saw a place in the world for me and was excited for me to see it too.

The *aha moment* of recognizing my personal, uncharted potential was monumental for my life course. It was as if I had found magic. From then on, I craved any information that would help me know how to work that magic. That day changed my life.

As a grownup, I always wanted to thank Miss Bingham. Sadly, I could never locate her. She only taught at Miller Elementary for one year and then moved away to start her family.

As a tribute to her, I named the teacher in my *Spencer's Adventures* series, Miss Bingham. After several books in the series were published, I received a letter from Susan Churchward. It wasn't until I started to read the letter that I realized Susan Churchward was Miss Bingham's married name. It was a wonderful, heartfelt letter. It was eight pages long because she could vividly remember some of the things I did in her class many years ago.

I was excited to write her back and let her know how she changed my life. I thanked her for listening to my crazy ideas and jokes. I detailed what a difference she made in my life story and how I often talked about her while addressing teacher conferences. I let her know that her influence as a teacher is a part of every book I write.

She wrote me right back, "Thanks for saying all the wonderful things but I'm not sure how they can be true. It was my first year teaching, and I wasn't sure I was doing it right. It seemed to me like the kids didn't even listen that year."

I wrote back, "I listened. Love, Gary."

I spent the same amount of my life with my first-grade teacher as I did with Miss Bingham. One of those teachers judged me, while the other one listened to me. One of them changed my life, and I can't remember the other one's name.

Crystals congregate to form an icy window frame for a mountain stream. The water adjusts to reveal a mosaic of stone. Nature is the constant creator. It is a symphony of moving parts continually seeking balance and order. You were given the endowment of imagination, a rare commodity among living creatures. It is your invitation to contribute to this never-ending tapestry of life.

Find your colors.
Discover your voice.
Pick up your tools.
Share your life.

grow

The art of becoming is everyone's destiny. We are all servants to the process of change. No one can temper time or diminish their age. However, we can determine our direction. Your heart is fertile ground designed to nurture growth. In your never-ceasing journey of becoming, listen to your heart. It has a quiet voice. Slow down, tune in, and discover which direction you should grow.

Lost in Seoul

Traveling is one of the best ways for a child to gain confidence. They learn to manage unexpected challenges, understand social differences, and become more aware of their surroundings. These three qualities can help a young person develop life skills that offer clarity in uncertain times.

When I was invited to spend three days presenting school assemblies and writing workshops at Taejon Christian International School in South Korea, I invited my fifteen-year-old daughter, Annie, to join me. As we waited for our international flight in Los Angeles, she was feeling apprehensive about what we would encounter in South Korea.

"What if I don't like the food?" asked Annie.

"What if you do?" I replied.

"What happens if we get lost?" she asked.

"I'll be surprised if we don't get lost," I said.

"We can't understand the language. How will we be able to communicate?" asked Annie.

"The most important word we need to know is *kamsahamnida*. That's how you say thank you in Korean," I explained.

Annie practiced saying *kamsahamnida* while we waited for our flight. By the time we boarded the plane, she could pronounce it perfectly.

Our first challenge came at Incheon International Airport upon landing in Seoul late at night. After collecting our luggage, we exited the airport.

"How are we going to get to our hotel?" asked Annie.

"On a bus," I said.

The street was humming with buses, taxis, and shuttles. It was fast and loud, and everyone was in an enormous hurry. We walked up and down the sidewalk several times while I tried to figure out which bus would take us to the part of the city where our hotel was.

"Which one should we get on?" asked Annie nervously.

"I have no idea," I answered, as I turned around and headed back into the airport.

I located an information booth and made a beeline for it. I handed the attendant my hotel reservation and asked if she would print the name of the hotel and address in Korean for us. She was happy to oblige.

"Kamsahamnida," said Annie.

Back outside, I handed the paper to a bus driver. He read it and then pointed out which bus we needed to take to get to the right neighborhood. As we boarded that bus, I showed the paper to our driver. After reading it, he showed me on a map which bus stop was closest to our hotel.

After we sat down, Annie said, "I was really nervous back there."

"I was too. I felt totally lost," I confessed. "That's why I headed back into the airport. I've been in lots of airports and know they all have information booths. I should have stopped at the booth before we left the airport the first time, but I was distracted by all the new sights and sounds."

The next day we took the train to Daejeon, South Korea, where Taejon Christian International School is located. The principal, George Zickefoose, greeted us at the train station in Daejeon and took us to a small apartment where we would be staying during our days at his school.

The next morning, we met Barbara Boyer. She was the librarian and had drawn up a full schedule of presentations for the next three days. The teachers were wonderful, and the students were some of the most respectful children I have ever met. The older students particularly loved meeting Annie. They were all curious about what her school was like back in Utah.

When our visit to Taejon Christian International School was over, I had scheduled two days for Annie and me to experience the sights and culture of Seoul, South Korea.

The morning of our first day in Seoul, I told Annie that she was completely in charge of transportation. I wanted her to gain the confidence and experience of using the subway system in a large city.

"But what if I get us lost?" she nervously asked.

"We'll just reverse our steps until we get to a place that we are familiar with and begin again. Just like we did at the airport on the night we arrived," I answered.

We made our way to the subway station near our hotel, and Annie looked at a map on the wall.

"Where are we going?" she asked.

"Namdaemun Market," I replied.

Barbara Boyer had given me a list of attractions she thought we would enjoy in Seoul. Namdaemun Market was at the top of her list. This massive shopping district is the largest and oldest shopping experience in South Korea. It has existed for over six hundred years and today has more than 10,000 different vendors.

"We need to get to Hoehyeon Station on Subway Line 4," said Annie.

"Lead the way," I said.

Annie's navigational skills turned out to be right on. In less than half an hour, we were walking out of Hoehyeon Station near Namdaemun Market. I quickly surmised that this would be an extremely easy place to get lost. Worried that we might have a tough time finding our way back to the subway station, I told Annie to look up and pick out a landmark.

"A what?" she asked.

"Choose something that is high enough that you can see it from a distance," I advised. "It will let us know where the station is if we get lost."

Annie's gaze moved across the tops of the buildings. Near the entrance of the subway station were various billboards attached to the top of a tall building.

"Got it," she said. "I picked the billboard with the cute guy on it. Trust me, I will not forget him."

Namdaemun Market is a sprawling maze. It was shopping on a scale like nothing I had ever experienced. There was shop after shop, on top of shop after shop, next to shop after shop, and on and on and on. After more than two hours, we were both exhausted from the merchandise overload. Like two tired bees, we had lost our shopping buzz.

"Dad, I'm sick of this," said Annie.

"Me too," I said. "Let's go back to the hotel. Can you get us to the subway station?"

"It's right down this street," said Annie.

I sighed and said, "Lead the way."

That street did not lead to Hoehyeon Station. For close to an hour, I followed as Annie took us down one street after another without making any headway. We were lost in Seoul.

Finally, in frustration, Annie stopped and said, "I give up. I do not know where we are or how to get us to the subway station."

"Annie, when are you ever going to look up?" I asked.

She raised her eyes and immediately spotted the billboard with the cute young man.

"Follow me," she said with newfound confidence.

Using her landmark as a guide, Annie had us back at Hoehyeon Station in less than ten minutes. On the subway ride back to the hotel, I congratulated Annie for being a good navigator.

"You call getting us lost for an hour being a good navigator?" asked Annie. "I totally forgot about the landmark until you gave me a clue."

"We all get lost or feel confused at times. I felt that way the night we were trying to get on the bus at the airport. It's not a big deal if you learn something from the experience that can help you in the future," I said. "Did you learn something?"

"Don't forget to look up," she said.

It has been many years since our adventure in South Korea. Annie is a smart, successful woman who loves to travel. I recently asked her if she still remembered what she learned that day at Namdaemun Market.

"My phone has a GPS, so I don't get lost anymore," she said with a laugh. "But the life lesson you taught me that day I use all the time. I make emotional landmarks by memorizing how I feel when I have accomplished something significant. When I feel discouraged, I look above my doubts and frustrations and recall how my achievement made me feel. In my mind, I retrace the steps I took to reach that goal. It usually gets me back on track."

In my office, I have a shadow box that Annie made with some of our souvenirs from our trip to South Korea. Lining the back of the box is the subway map she used to guide us to Namdaemun Market. It is the perfect backdrop for our adventure. All of Annie's trepidations about the trip came true. She didn't like the food. She couldn't understand the language. She certainly spent time being lost. And according to her, it was one of the best experiences of her life. *Kamsahamnida.*

clarity

Confusion is the fuzzy feeling of doubt that accompanies not knowing. It can accelerate worries and freeze intentions. Replacing *what if* with *I can* is the first step for clarity. *What if* a decision ends up being wrong? *You can* handle it. *You can* apologize. *You can* learn from it. Stop overthinking. Quit second-guessing. Seeing your way forward requires decisiveness. Clarity isn't a crystal ball that allows you to always be right. It's a feeling that you can always be strong.

BUILD

Life is a complicated puzzle full of interconnecting pieces. Keeping up with relationships, obligations, demands, desires, feelings, and commitments can leave you feeling scattered. Use your heart as the source of your strength. It has the power to help you bridge a gap, pick up the slack, hold up your end, keep your word, and build a relationship.

Swimming Lessons

I hated swimming lessons. The small town of Burley, Idaho, had one outdoor swimming pool when I was growing up. Swimming lessons were held early in the morning, so they didn't interfere with the pool's regular hours for public swimming. It was always cold, and the wind was often blowing. If you weren't in the water, you were shivering in the cool Southern Idaho breeze. It wasn't fun, and I failed every swimming test I ever took. The best I could do was the doggie paddle.

I took swimming lessons because my mom wanted me to, and I loved my mom. As an eleven-year-old, I was still in the swimming class with the six and seven-year-olds. It was embarrassing.

I was standing in the shallow end of the pool with a bunch of first and second graders when the instructor motioned for me to get out of the pool.

"I'm going to have you switch classes," said the teenager, who was the instructor.

He pointed to a group of kids that were lined up at the diving board at the other end of the pool. "Go be with them," said the teenager.

I hurried to the diving board and joined the boys and girls who were waiting in line. I was still older than these kids, but being short for my age, it looked like I fit in with them.

"What are you doing here?" asked the teenage girl who was teaching this more advanced class.

I pointed to the other instructor and said, "He told me to join this group."

"OK, whatever," said the girl. "We are going to go off the diving boards today."

Burley's pool had two diving boards, a low dive, and a high dive. We lined up at the low dive, and one by one, we walked the plank and plunked into the water. A couple of the boys tried to be hot dogs and attempted to dive, but both efforts ended in loud belly flops. I walked to the end of the board, closed my eyes, and dropped into the water. It was fun. I doggie paddled to the side of the pool and was eager to try again. We each got one more turn before the instructor blew her whistle and ordered us to line up at the high dive.

I am terrified of heights. I gulped and looked up at the board twelve feet above me. I found a spot at the end of the line and watched the other kids take their turns. My plan was to close my eyes, and try not to scream as I dropped into the water.

When it was my turn, I bravely walked to the end of the rough-feeling board. Just before I was going to step off into the air, I changed my mind, and my toes gripped the end of the diving board. I stood there looking down at the water while the instructor blew her whistle.

The other kids started encouraging me, which made matters worse. The instructor blew her whistle again, louder this time. On the third shrill blast from the whistle, I decided that I didn't have to risk my life for her. I turned around and walked back to the ladder.

I was about to take the first step down the ladder when I looked at the chain link fence surrounding the pool. Standing there was my hero and best friend. My dad had arrived just in time to see me chickening out. I didn't wave. I didn't smile. I just stared at him.

"Make like a frog and jump off that thing," said my dad, smiling.

To me, that was the greatest pep talk ever given. No cheerleading. No promises of a reward. No threats. No belittling. In nine words, he simplified the task at hand. He didn't ask me to have the courage of a lion or soar like an eagle. I just needed to be as brave as a frog. I could do that.

I turned around, walked to the other end of the board, closed my eyes, and dropped. With my arms flailing, I hit the water. By the time I doggie paddled to the side of the pool and climbed out, the other kids were lining up for a second jump. I got in line and kept looking to see where my dad was. But he was already gone.

When I got home, my dad never mentioned the diving board incident and neither did I. It was already in the past. My dad knew I wasn't a chicken. He had watched me ride bucking horses. We roped steers together. He was the one who told me that I didn't need to tell Mom every detail about what we were doing because she would blame him for putting me in dangerous situations.

Obviously, I wasn't going to be a great swimmer or an Olympic diver, and Dad was fine with that. There were plenty of things I was good at, and I didn't need to feel bad about the things that I couldn't do well.

The next day, my new class had our final swimming test. The backstroke was first on the list. Since I had never tried a backstroke in my life, I ended up at the bottom of the pool. It was a fitting conclusion to the last swimming lesson of my life.

The next week, I went to a pond and caught a tadpole. I put it in one of my mom's glass bowls with a big rock and placed it on the dresser in my room. For many weeks, I watched its metamorphosis. It first grew some back legs. Some weeks later, the front legs appeared. Eventually the tail began to shrink, and then it disappeared. One morning I watched as it jumped off the rock into the water like it was no big deal. After all the amazing changes it had gone through, it was just a regular little frog that did ordinary frog things.

I set the frog free near the canal that runs through our farm. I watched him hop into the water and swim away. That was the same canal where I ended up learning to swim later that same summer. I taught myself. It was no big deal. It turns out I didn't hate swimming. I hated swimming lessons. Some of my favorite memories as a teenager are of my friends and me swimming in that canal.

I've always been grateful that my mom made me take those early morning swimming lessons. They were a part of my metamorphosis from boy to young man. I didn't learn how to swim, but I did figure out that doing something embarrassing or scary for someone you love is what grownups do. That is a lesson that has helped me in my life much more than the backstroke.

stretch

We all have comfort zones, safe havens where we feel emotionally secure. While hunkering down in bunkers of familiar means and manners offers security, it also limits range of motion. Stiffening your heart creates resistance to new ideas. Your heart is an emotional muscle that requires daily stretching. Widen your stance, reach outside of your comfort zone, and stand up for yourself.

moments

A bubble in a stream holds its shape for as long as possible, but change is unavoidable. It morphs and wiggles but undoubtedly will disappear into the expanse of the moving water. Its fleeting existence only increases the marvel of its presence. The menagerie of moments that comprise your life is precious. They testify to your existence. Hold them in your consciousness. Share them and love them. You will move along with the stream of time soon enough.

Blue Sky

I find ten-year-olds to be some of the most candid people on the planet. They are socially aware but not to the extent that they feel self-conscious about expressing their true feelings. This can be good or bad, but it is always interesting.

I was visiting a fourth-grade classroom when, during a Q&A session, a girl named Rachel yelled out the question, "What's your net worth?"

I shrugged and honestly replied, "I have no idea."

The teacher interjected, "Rachel, it's not polite to ask such personal questions. Ask Mr. Hogg questions about his books and how he writes them."

As I answered some of the other students' questions, I noticed that Rachel had sneaked a phone out of her desk and that both of her thumbs were quickly typing. When she raised her head, she loudly announced, "He doesn't have any net worth. I just googled it."

The teacher was clearly embarrassed.

"What does that mean?" asked a boy in the back of the room.

"It means he doesn't have any money," answered Rachel, using her most dramatic voice.

A collective sigh of sympathy from the students filled the room. And then questions and comments came flooding my way.

"Do you live in a house?" asked a boy in the front row.

"How do you buy food?" asked another student.

"I'm going to tell my mom to buy all of your books," said a girl from the back of the room.

I laughed and said, "You are all truly kind to worry about me, but I am not living in poverty." I then discussed the difference between net worth and self-worth.

Contributing to the well-being of those around us is a vital element of self-worth. Often, students are the ones who remind me of this important concept. Jake was one of those students.

After a writing workshop with a class of creative fourth-grade students in Amarillo, Texas, the students gathered to have me autograph their writing journals. While I was signing the notebooks, I spotted a boy waiting off to the side. His clothes were far from being new, and his cowboy boots were well worn. While other students were shoving papers at me to sign, he patiently waited his turn.

When the crowd had dispersed, he came over and handed me his journal. As I signed it, he said, "Mr. Hogg, thank you for being my blue sky."

His sincerity took me by surprise. I wasn't sure I had heard him correctly.

"Excuse me?" I said.

In a louder voice, he said, "You were my blue sky today."

"I think you have it backwards," I said. "You're making me feel like I'm under a blue sky. Thank you for your kind words."

I asked him his name and we visited for a minute while the other students hurried out to recess. After Jake left, I saw that Ms. Chew, the school's principal, was standing nearby, waiting to talk to me. I approached her and asked if she had noticed the boy I had been visiting with.

"I know that boy very well," she said.

"He just told me that I was his blue sky. That might be the kindest compliment I've ever received," I said.

With emotion in her voice, Ms. Chew said, "Oh, Gary, if you only knew how many dark days that boy has."

"Well, he certainly brightened my day today," I replied.

After that day in Amarillo, I challenge students at the schools I visit to create blue-sky atmospheres in their classrooms. I encourage them to share smiles, compliments, and kind words with each other and their teachers.

During an assembly program in Mesa, Arizona, I was in the middle of issuing the blue-sky challenge when a ten-year-old blurted out in a loud voice, "I don't want to be anyone's blue sky."

The other students' heads quickly turned to get a look at the bold boy.

"Are you having a bad day?" I asked.

"I'm having a very bad day," was his immediate response.

"Whenever I'm having a horrible day, I find someone I can share something with, give a compliment to, tell a joke to, or just smile at. It helps them have a little blue sky," I said.

And then I asked the most important question of the day, "Who gets to stand under the same blue sky with them?"

"You do," grumbled the boy.

"You should try it," I concluded.

For the rest of the day, I was in individual classrooms conducting writing workshops. During the last workshop, I caught sight of someone waving at me through the open door. I looked over and saw the boy who was having a difficult day. He was grinning from ear to ear as he gave me a thumbs-up. He had obviously found his blue sky by creating a little blue sky for someone else.

Self-worth should never be confused with net worth. We are all rich enough to smile, say kind words, offer sincere compliments, encourage a loved one, and share with a stranger. Be someone's blue sky today.

connect

The road of your life is full of unanticipated meetings. Step by step and choice by choice you're moving closer to meeting someone you have no idea exists. At an unexpected moment, your footprints will align. In an instant you'll decide to engage or move on. Stop rushing. Invoke a little patience. Connections are made by listening. Friendships are built on common ground. The discovery of a kindred heart is worth the effort.

WORDS

Whether written or spoken, words are at the epicenter of humanity. They form the backbone of promises, and the foundation of lies. The words you choose coupled with your actions expose your character. Use your heart to choose words that truly align with your best self. Whether read by millions or whispered to a friend, the words you choose contribute to the conversation of life that connects us all.

The Reward for Being Brave

There is something about the courage of a first grader that is astonishing to me. Every day, they learn new ideas and ways of doing things. They follow directions. They raise their hands to participate. They discover that they don't always have to have a turn. They are taught not to tattle. They are incredible human beings.

Why does that kind of courage seem to evaporate the older we get? By the time brave first graders get to junior high school, many of them have traded in their brave cards for magnifying glasses. Where before, they wouldn't have given a second thought to how they appeared to their peers, they now overthink each of their actions. They seek approval instead of courage.

Standing on a gym floor in New Mexico, I was looking up at bleachers that were packed with high school students. I was trying to get the students to participate in a brainstorm as part of a writing workshop.

One of the first to raise his hand was a stout football player wearing a varsity jacket. Before I could call on him, he looked over to his friend. His friend's arms were folded, and he had a disinterested expression on his face. The football player lowered his arm and joined his friend in an act of apathy.

As I watched him lower his arm, I thought, *Why did you need to run your courage through your friend before you could use it? Why does that guy get to have control over the effort you give?*

It's interesting that some people often just need a disapproving look or the tiniest negative comment to undermine their resolve. The danger in living this way is that you are giving a degree of power to people who may not have your best interests at heart. It can lead to living an anxious, approval-seeking life.

The reward for being brave is that you're brave. You don't need a compliment, certificate, pat on the back, or a certain number of likes on your social media to feel significant.

When my daughter, Annie, was in high school, I was walking past her bedroom door and I heard her crying. I cracked the door and asked what was wrong.

"I'm OK," was her tearful response.

"Clearly, you're not," I said as I walked over and put my arm around her shoulder.

"Jonah said something that made me feel bad," she said.

"Where is he?" I asked.

Annie could tell I was going to get in the middle of their disagreement.

"No, Dad, don't say anything," pleaded Annie.

"But you're crying," I said.

"I want to be part of the solution for us to have a happy family, not part of the problem," said Annie. "I can figure it out and find a way to resolve it. I'll talk to Jonah myself."

"I want to help," I offered.

"If it was a really big deal, I'd talk to you, but this is an argument and we have to figure it out ourselves," said Annie.

Annie could have used her tears to gain an advantage over her brother. She could have cast blame and been manipulative. Instead, she chose to share her courage, not her criticism. She stood up for herself without putting Jonah down.

Our modern world is full of instant judgments and critical attitudes. Living your best life requires you to declare your independence and take responsibility for yourself. Just like you did in first grade, raise your hand, follow directions, don't tattle, take your turn, learn something new, and be brave.

authentic

Shadows are created when an image blocks a source of light. Differing angles of the light can exaggerate or minimize features of the image. The object doesn't change, the intensity and direction of the luminous source creates the distortion. You are an authentic soul. Your measure should not be determined by another's light. Comparing and contrasting ourselves with others can be emotional fetters. Live a bona fide life true to your own inner light.

There is only one you in all of the galaxies. The elements that comprise your physical body are plentiful, but the unexplainable concoction of sensitivities that creates the essence of your spirit is unprecedented. Never let mundane matters muddle the value of your life. You are a rare creature, and we are honored to know you.

The Deep Dive

My biggest joy in life is being a father. When my son Jackson turned fourteen, I was looking for an adventure that the two of us could do together. My cousin Stan had just gotten certified in scuba diving and suggested that it would be something that Jackson would love. He was right. Jackson took his first swimming lesson before he could walk. On top of that, he was fascinated by all marine life. He considered manatees his brothers.

Scuba diving was not on my bucket list. My lackluster swimming skills combined with my horrific seasickness tendencies make me a terrible candidate for the underwater activity.

Good fathers put their kids before their fears, so despite my inadequacies, I signed us up with Hans, a local scuba instructor. We attended the classes, did the worksheets, and passed the tests. After completing the two required open-water dives, we were certified scuba divers.

Stan was eager to have us go with him on a diving experience. He invited us several times over the next year to join him on one of his scuba trips. I turned him down each time. My problem was my seaworthiness. I have always struggled with motion sickness. The idea of being on a boat in the ocean for a significant amount of time was a deal breaker for me.

"Are we ever going to go on a scuba trip?" asked Jackson.

"Of course," I answered. "I just need to find a place where we don't have to be on a boat all day."

The next summer, Stan called and announced, "I found a place in Mexico that is just the ticket for you. It is less than a fifteen minute boat ride and the diving is out of this world."

"That sounds perfect," I said. "Let's stay for a whole week."

Jackson nearly flipped out when I gave him the news. We rented a condominium on the beach and reserved dive times with the local dive shop. The first dive was scheduled for the second morning of our trip.

We met divemaster José at his dive shop at seven a.m. He was an easy-going fellow in his early forties. We picked up the scuba gear and made our way onto a deck to get ready for the dive.

We were diving with a family of six adults from Texas who were experienced divers. They were a fun and rowdy group that loved to goof around. As a joke, one of the men even insisted on diving in his Wrangler jeans. They kept José occupied while our little group prepared for the early morning dive.

It had been over a year since we had completed our training, and I was fuzzy on some of the technical aspects. The basic equipment of scuba diving includes a mask, regulator, air tank, snorkel, buoyancy control vest, fins, a wet suit, and a weight belt. The weight belt is a thick nylon strap, and the diver slides lead weights onto it. The amount of weight is determined by the wet suit's thickness, the air tank's size, and the diver's body weight. I had no idea how many weights to slide onto my belt.

"How many of these weights do I need?" I asked Stan.

"It's better to have too many than not enough," answered Stan.

I decided to err on the side of too much and slid a long row of weights onto my belt.

The boat ride was short. In a little over ten minutes, we were at the diving location. With a loud yee-haw, the cowboy in the Wranglers was over the side of the boat. The other Texans quickly stampeded into the water behind him.

I felt my heart rate accelerate as I dropped off the side of the boat. I was beyond nervous as I bobbed in the water. My apprehensive attitude was replaced with courage when I saw the huge smile on Jackson's face. My goal was to stay as close to my son as possible throughout the dive.

Due to the weight I had on my belt, I began going down much faster than the other divers. While they stopped to equalize their ears, I sank right past them. I felt pressure in my right ear and then a sharp pain. I tried to slow my descent, but like a human anchor, I kept sinking. To use a bad pun, I was in way over my head.

I began kicking as hard as I could. My quick descent slowed down, but I wasn't any closer to making my way back to the group. At this point, I had no idea how far down I was or where the other divers were. I was disoriented and lost in the sea.

Don't panic, I thought. I knew if I freaked out, it would be a disaster of epic proportions. The only way I could keep this from happening was to get control of my breathing. I was concentrating on slowing my breaths when I felt a hard tug on my weight belt. It was divemaster José. He unhooked my weight belt, slid off the first weight, and let it fall.

José dropped weight after weight until there were only a couple of them left on the belt. He then slid the end of the belt back into the buckle and secured it. Looking me in the eye, he gave me the demand-response signal, which is the OK sign.

I returned a shaky OK sign, and we both swam up to where the other divers were. None of them had even realized that I had disappeared. Divemaster José had just saved my life, and we were the only two who knew it.

This is the part of the story I wish I could say everything from that point on was magical. I want to write about the gorgeous sea life I witnessed. I wish I had had the time of my life. But that wouldn't be true.

The sharp pain I felt in my right ear was my eardrum popping, and some water got into my middle ear. It made me so dizzy that the entire ocean was spinning. During the rest of the dive, I stared at Jackson's flippers and tried my best to keep up. When we finally returned to the surface, I was so sick that I pulled out my mouthpiece and vomited.

I climbed into the boat, green faced and miserable. As the Texans spun tales of the incredible underwater world they had just witnessed, I fought back the urge to throw up.

"Are you OK?" asked Jackson.

"I'll be fine. I just need to get back to shore," I said. "Did you enjoy the dive?"

"It was amazing. I can't wait to go again," replied Jackson.

As soon as I got off the boat, I laid down in the warm sand and closed my eyes. While everyone else made their way back to José's dive shop, I relived the events of the morning in my mind. I had almost died, and it was my fault. Why did I put so much weight on my belt? How come I didn't seek out José's advice before the dive?

And then the life lesson from the near disaster came into focus for me. It was a metaphor for the life I was living. It had been two years since I had gone through a divorce, and I was still feeling the weight of it. The feelings of embarrassment, guilt, inadequacy, disappointment, and anger were heavy, and I took them all on. I carried them everywhere I went. That morning on the beach, I realized it was too much. I was drowning.

Just like José unbuckled my belt to get rid of unnecessary weight, I opened my heart and began to lighten my load. I was in control of the weight belt. I dropped the weight of shame. I let go of resentment. I slid off the heaviness of other people's expectations. I unburdened myself from holding grudges. I released the feeling of not being good enough. I let them all fall to the bottom of the sea.

I pictured myself rising. I felt lighter, younger, and more hopeful than I had in a long time. That day was the beginning, not the end. I still sometimes get disappointed, worry too much, or feel inadequate. But now those feelings are temporary. I can let them go.

A worker from the dive shop came out and told me that José said I had to get off the beach. I was bad for business. He didn't want other people to think that people got sick on his dive trips.

I got up and made my way to the dive shop. José was waiting for me. He wasted no time in telling me that I was the worst diver he had ever taken out on a dive. When he was finished listing all of my inadequacies, I shook his hand and said, "Thank you for saving my life."

He gripped my hand and said, "That is what I was there for."

José was a hero that day. He noticed that I was gone. He immediately set out to find me. He quickly recognized the problem. He didn't waste time rectifying it. He made sure I was OK. He didn't embarrass me in front of the group. That is what heroes do.

Raising children is an adventure we get to share with them. Children need their fathers to be heroes. In a moment, they can get in over their heads and need a dad who is willing to dive deep to keep them safe. By letting go of unnecessary emotional baggage, I was more qualified to be that hero. While scuba diving is something I'll never do again, that trip to Mexico accomplished what I hoped it would. It made me a better father.

Balancing your intentions with your endeavors requires the consistency that peace offers. A peaceful heart quickens your joy. It unclutters your thoughts. It expands your possibilities. It deepens your understanding. Finding harmony in your soul that transcends the noise of your existence is not the end destination. It is the starting point.

Sucker branches grow on a tree in response to stress or injury. These unsightly limbs steal water and nutrients that the tree needs for healthy growth. Emotional wounds can cause twigs of turmoil to sprout in our hearts, diverting energy needed for happiness into frustration, anger, and destructive habits. You can't go back in time and change what you've done or what others have done to you, but you can forgive. Releasing resentment and regrets is liberating. It frees your soul to grow in new healthy and loving directions.

Relationship Advice from Second Graders

I had been a single dad for more than ten years when I met Emily. Our mutual friend Angie introduced us and insisted that we go out on a date. I invited Emily on a horseback ride up the mountain trail near my house. We had a fun time moseying up the trail while we were getting to know each other. After the ride, Emily said she wasn't looking to date anyone but would like to be friends.

"That works for me," I said. "We can be saddle pals."

And that's how our friendship began. It was a fun summer being friends with Emily. We didn't end up going on many more horseback rides, but we did go on hikes and trail runs. She had two smart, wonderful sons, Ethan and Benjamin. I loved getting to know them. I found them to be strong, independent, and creative boys.

As life unfolds, sometimes love finds you when you aren't looking for it. That was the case with us. One year later, I asked Emily to be my bride. We decided to have the ceremony in Carlsbad, California, in a park that overlooks the Pacific Ocean. We wanted to keep it a small affair and only invited our immediate families.

In San Diego County, friends or family members can perform marriage ceremonies with a special one-day certification that can be purchased from the county office. It felt natural to have one of our children perform the marriage ceremony. We asked Jackson, who was twenty-five at the time, if he would do the honors.

Naturally, it was the best wedding I have ever attended. Jackson's talk was insightful and inspiring. His tender words had everyone teary eyed. From that moment on we have been a loving and united family. Our kids all get along and love each other, and Emily is my forever sweetheart.

Eleven years later, on a camping trip in the Sawtooth National Forest of Idaho, Jackson accompanied me on an evening hike. As we walked, he looked over at me and said, "It's time for you to pay me back."

"OK," I said. "What are you talking about?"

"I married you and Emily. I want you to return the favor and marry me and Chelbie," said Jackson.

"It will be my honor," I said as I gave him a hug.

I had never married anyone before, and I wanted my remarks to be fitting for such a sacred event. More has been written about love than any other literary theme. Contributing something new on the subject was a tall order. William Shakespeare penned my personal favorite description of love in his Sonnet 116.

Love is not love
Which alters when it alteration finds,
Or bends with the remover to remove.
O no! it is an ever-fixed mark
That looks on tempests and is never shaken;
It is the star to every wand'ring bark.

I had to find profound words that would describe ways for Jackson and Chelbie to honor the ever-fixed mark that Shakespeare wrote about. I needed help and knew just who to ask.

I was teaching writing workshops at Las Positas Elementary School in La Habra, California, during the days leading up to the ceremony. During the conclusion of my workshop with second graders, I asked for advice.

While I was explaining about the wedding, tiny hands started to go in the air. It turned out that these children had some strong feelings about how to keep love alive in a relationship. These are the responses I used in the wedding ceremony. They are written just as the students said them.

Don't stay on your phone all the time like my dad does.
Make goo-goo eyes at each other.
Don't be shy to ask.
Take a deep breath.
Make funny jokes.
Talk to each other instead of texting.
Pick up your own stuff.
Be fair.
Don't fight over the small things.
Live a grateful life.

These seven-year-old boys and girls offered some of the best relationship advice I have ever heard. They are the perfect companion words to Shakespeare's sonnet. He outlined the lofty goal of love, and these kids gave me the nitty gritty of how to show someone you love them.

Jackson and Chelbie's wedding was a magical day that I will always remember. It was inspiring to be a part of them promising their hearts and lives to each other. It made me think of that day in May when I pledged my love to Emily. We started off as two saddle pals who became eternal companions. Our love is my ever-fixed mark. And because of that love, I live a grateful life.

Love is consistent in kindness.
Love makes heartache bearable.
Love puts meaning into sacrifice.
Love lifts joy out of the ordinary.
Love offers unity through grace.
Love holds on when doubts arise.
Love understands imperfection.
Love builds confidence through trust.
Love offers rest and gives space.
Love is your greatest superpower.

VOICE

You are the author of your life story. Your time on this planet is your notebook and your heart holds the ink. Only by opening your heart can you let your life's possibilities flow out. Purpose will give your story power, and details will give it tenderness. Your author's voice is needed today. We need to know what is important to you. We need to hear your call for kindness and see your honest actions.

Children's Books by Gary Hogg

Happy Hawk Golden Thought Picture Books
I Heard of a Nerd Bird
Friendship in the Forest
Lizzie Learns about Lying
Sir William the Worm
The Half-hearted Hare
The Lion Who Couldn't Roar

Spencer's Adventures Chapter Books
Stop That Eyeball!
Garbage Snooper Surprise
Hair in the Air
The Great Toilet Paper Caper
Let Go of That Toe
Don't Bake That Snake

Charlie Bacon Chapter Books
Bears Scares and Underwear
Help! My Dad is the Lunch Lady
Beware of the Cheese Princess
Welcome to Zombie School
The Dreaded Snowman Wedgie
King of Turkey Town
The Fantastic Dragon Catcher
Wiener Dog of Doom
The Great Unicorn Roundup

Also by Gary Hogg
Look What the Car Dragged In
Beautiful Buehla and the Zany Zoo Makeover
Scrambled Eggs and Spider Legs

About the Author

Gary Hogg has been writing stories since he was a boy growing up in Burley, Idaho. His many children's books have been read and loved by millions. Gary is a popular speaker who has presented at more than three thousand schools and conferences. Two million students have participated in his writing workshops. Gary lives in Huntsville, Utah with his wife Emily. They are the parents of six talented and kind children. To learn more about Gary Hogg's books and speaking engagements visit garyhoggbooks.com.

connect
laugh
peace
heal
hymn
grit